Conversations with J. K. Rowling

Conversations with

J. K. ROWLING

By Lindsey Fraser

Scholastic Inc.

New York   Toronto   London   Auckland   Sydney

Mexico City   New Delhi   Hong Kong   Buenos Aires

Library of Congress Cataloging-in-Publication Data Available

ISBN 0-439-31455-0   LC number 2001029392

10 9 8 7 6 5 4 3 2   01 02 03 04 05

Book design by David Saylor

Printed in the U.S.A.

First edition, October 2001

With many thanks to the Harry Potter aficionados of
Crailing, Durham Road, and Gifford.
—L. F.

CONTENTS

An Interview with J. K. Rowling

J. K. Rowling's Books

Conversations with J. K. Rowling

MY FAMILY AND
MY CHILDHOOD

Where did you come in the family?

I was the older of two girls. My earliest memory is of my sister being born—she's just under two years younger than me. My dad gave me Play-Doh the day she arrived, to keep me occupied while he ran in and out of the bedroom. I have no memory of seeing the new baby, but I do remember eating the Play-Doh.

Were books important in your family?

Another early memory is of having the measles—I must have been about four—and Dad reading *The Wind in the Willows*. I don't remember feeling ill at all—just lying there listening to those stories. Both my parents loved reading. My mother was a huge reader—she was quite bookish—and never happier than when she was curled up, reading. That was a big influence on me. She came from a family of teachers and I think my dad followed her example.

Tell us about your grandparents.

My grandfathers were called Ernie and Stanley—I named the driver and conductor of the Knight Bus which comes to rescue Harry Potter after them. They were both great characters. Ernie owned a supermarket, and when we went to stay—they lived in a flat above the shop—he would let my sister and me play shops after hours with real tins and packets and money. Just as long as we put everything back.

Stanley sometimes had a problem telling fact from fiction. He was a great dreamer, and spent a lot of time in his garden shed, making things.

One of my grandmothers was called Kathleen—my middle name. I adored her, and my saddest memory of that time is of her death. My other grandmother was obsessed with dogs, which she much preferred to humans. There was a touch of Aunt Marge in her, to tell the truth.

Did you have any pets?

When I was very, very tiny we had a dog called Thumper, named after the rabbit in the Disney film, *Bambi*. I was very sad when he was put down. We had two guinea pigs later on, but they were eaten by a fox. I remember the scene of carnage on the back lawn—it was not pleasant. . . . And we had another dog, Misty, who was around until after I went to university.

As a teenager I had tropical fish. That was a big hobby and I still love them.

Where were you born?

In Chipping Sodbury near Bristol. I'm very proud of that! I think it probably doomed me to a love of weird place-names. Until I was about nine we lived in and around Bristol, and then we moved to Tutshill, a little village near Chepstow in South Wales. It is a town dominated by a castle on a cliff, which might explain a lot.

Why did you move to the country?

I think it was really a dream of my parents', both of whom had urban childhoods. They met on a train heading north to Scotland from Kings Cross Station in London. Dad was in the navy and Mum was a Wren [Women's Royal Naval Service] and they were both traveling to a posting in Arbroath, just north of Dundee. It was love at first sight; they married at nineteen and had me at twenty. They both dreamed of life in a country cottage, and my dad could commute easily from Chepstow to his work at the Rolls Royce factory.

Tell us about the place where you lived.

Our house was a cottage next to the church. It had originally been the village school. All our friends thought it was spooky living next to a graveyard but we liked it. I still love graveyards— they are a great source of names. We lived near Offa's Dyke on the River Wye—a wonderful place. We used to love exploring amongst the boulders.

When we got older, of course, it became boring. There wasn't as much to interest teenagers.

What else do you remember from that time?

One of my happiest memories is of a family

holiday in Norfolk. I am very close to my sister now, but when we were younger we fought like cat and dog. For some reason we were getting on unnaturally well during that holiday, and I just remember all the late-night laughing, the stories and jokes. I think my parents were surprised but relieved.

MY SCHOOL DAYS

What do you remember about your time at school?

My first school was on the outskirts of Bristol and I absolutely loved it, although I remember on my first day, when Mum came to pick me up for lunch, I thought that was it and that I'd "done" school and wouldn't need to go back.

The village school in Tutshill was pretty Dickensian—a complete contrast to the open-plan school I was used to. We were seated according to the teacher's perception of our brightness, and after ten minutes she put me in the "dim" row. There are a number of people who influenced the character of Snape in my books, and that teacher was definitely one of them. I found it extremely scary. We used to have The Daily Ten—mental arithmetic—and on my first day I got half a point. Well, I'd never done fractions before! I think that I grew on that teacher in time, but I remember having to work hard at it. And at the fractions.

What was your secondary school like?

I quite liked secondary school, but I was particularly influenced by my English teacher, Miss Shepherd. She was strict, and could be quite caustic, but she was very conscientious. I really respected her because she was a teacher who was passionate about teaching us. She was an introduction to a different kind of woman, I suppose. She was a feminist, and clever. She had this incredibly no-nonsense approach. I remember doodling while she was talking one day and she told me that I was being very rude indeed. I said, "But I'm listening," and she told me that I was still being rude. That really stuck with me. She never just said, "Don't do that." Her approach made far more of an impression. So I loved English. Miss Shepherd was very hot on structure and refused to allow us to be the least bit sloppy. Even though I read a great deal, it was very good to be shown exactly what gave writing structure and pace. I learned such a lot from her and we're still in touch. She was the only teacher I ever confided in. She inspired trust.

When *Harry Potter and the Philosopher's Stone* was published she sent me a letter via Bloomsbury, the publisher. Her comments meant more to me than any newspaper review, because I knew she would never have written anything unless she meant it. She was the personification of integrity. And she liked the book.

When I was in the Upper Sixth [corresponds to the twelfth grade in the American system] a very important thing happened. A boy called Seán Harris came to school, having been at school in

Cyprus—his dad was in the army. He became my best friend—*Harry Potter and the Chamber of Secrets* is dedicated to him.

He had a turquoise Ford Anglia which spelled freedom for me. When you live in a village in the country driving is very important. So you can imagine that I couldn't have just any old car rescuing Harry and Ron Weasley to take them to Hogwarts—it had to be a turquoise Ford Anglia. Ron Weasley isn't a living portrait of Seán, but he really is very Seán-ish.

It often isn't until I re-read what I've written that I realize where certain bits of my stories have come from. Harry was rescued by that car, just as the car rescued me from my boredom. It's one of the very few bits I can think of that have such a direct connection with real life. That, and when Harry looks in the mirror and sees his family waving to him. That was a very important image from my life, when I lost my mother.

Did you like all your teachers?

No, not all of them. My least favorite teacher was just a bully. I've met quite a few teachers now, both when I was teaching and when I've been visiting schools, and the bullies really do stand out. I understand from the teacher's point of view that it's very easy to be a bully, but it's also the worst, shabbiest thing you can do. We're back to Snape here.

Was there anything else you didn't like?

My least favorite subject was metalwork. I was the worst in my class—just terrible. I am not a practical person. . . . It seemed to me to be all about hammering stuff until I broke it. I did try, but I just could not do it. Mum always kept a ridiculous flat teaspoon I made which was useless, completely hopeless. I was terrible at woodwork too—I remember arriving home with a photograph frame composed mainly of glue.

I was also dreadful at sport, although I vaguely liked gym. I especially hated hockey. But I did like swimming and dancing.

And I loathed the uniform. It was brown and yellow, two colors I will now never, ever wear on principle.

Do you think your teachers thought you would become a writer?

I think Miss Shepherd might have believed I could be a writer but I don't think she expected it of me. I always, always wanted to be a writer but I *never* shared my burning ambition with anyone.

When I was about six I wrote a book—just a little story—and when I finished it I remember thinking, well now we can publish this. I wanted the complete experience, even then. I was a lot less arrogant by the time I was twenty-six. By then, I didn't think I had any chance whatsoever.

Can you describe what you were like as a child?

I think I was always very insecure, a real worrier, but I would put on a show of confidence to mask it. By eleven or twelve, I might just have been a tiny bit Hermione-ish. I always felt I had to achieve, my hand always had to be the first to go up, I always had to be right. Maybe it was because I felt quite plain in comparison to my sister. I probably felt I had to compensate.

I did relax as I got older which was a good thing, although I was still—and am still—a worrier. I was very lucky in having such good friends. That was especially important in my teens, when my mother became ill with multiple sclerosis. Anyone who has experienced something like this happening in their family will know the huge knock-on effect, and the stress involved. Friends become even more important, to talk to, to confide in.

What did you read?

I remember reading lots of Noddy with Mum. She was a great Enid Blyton fan. I'm not. I did read the Famous Five books, or at least some of them, but not much else.

I absolutely loved the Richard Scarry books. That first book I wrote aged six was a complete rip-off. I've kept some of those books from my childhood and my daughter loves them too.

I was completely horse-obsessed and had a picture book version of Anna Sewell's *Black Beauty* when I was about eight. I'd cry my eyes out at that story. I also read *Little Women* by Louisa May Alcott when I was eight, and that began my "Little Women Phase." I *was* Jo March for a few months.

But my favorite book was *The Little White Horse* by Elizabeth Goudge. It was probably something to do with the fact that the heroine was quite plain, but it is a very well-constructed and clever book, and the more you read it, the cleverer it appears. And perhaps more than any other book, it has a direct influence on the Harry Potter books. The author always included details of what her characters were eating and I remember liking that. You may have noticed that I always list the food being eaten at Hogwarts.

The important thing is that no book was ever forbidden or censored, except once, when, as a present, I'd been given a spin-off book from the TV program *The New Avengers*. It had a very violent beginning which disturbed me, and I was glad when Mum said—it was the only time she did—that I shouldn't read any more. Other than that we read anything. I read Jane Austen's *Pride and Prejudice* when I was eleven or twelve and *Vanity Fair* by William Thackeray when I was fourteen. I know that sounds precocious but it was there, so I read it.

I was like my mother—I'd read anything and everything. Even now, if I visit a strange bathroom in which someone has been inconsiderate enough not to have provided books to read, I'll read the labels on the toiletries.

I had an aunt who was a reader for the publishers Mills and Boon—she read manuscripts—and she would pass on those books too, so I'd read all these romantic novels in about one hour flat. I remember when I was nine reading my first James Bond novel—Ian Fleming's *Thunderball*—and being fascinated by the Bloody Marys they drank. There was something wonderful about a drink with tomato juice in it. I love Bloody Marys now. . . .

We were very, very lucky—we were bought lots of books.

Did you read poetry?

I must admit to having a slight blind spot

about poetry. I enjoyed the children's treasuries we had, but I don't think it could have been a great love of my mother's—and poetry isn't something I reach for now.

What do you enjoy reading now?

I love novels and biographies. I've got a bit of an obsession about the Kennedys—President John F. Kennedy's family. I started one of my book tours to America in Boston, and insisted on making a detour to visit the Kennedy Museum there. I was going on and on about the family to my driver until, just before we arrived, she told me that she'd dated Teddy Kennedy. The things she could have told me if I'd only given her the chance. . . .

My most influential writer, without a doubt, is Jessica Mitford. When my great-aunt gave me *Hons and Rebels* when I was fourteen she instantly became my heroine. She ran away from home to fight in the civil war in Spain, taking with her a camera that she had charged to her father's account. I wished I'd had the nerve to do something like that. She had tremendous moral courage and did some physically brave things as a human rights activist. I love her sense of humor, her great independence. She stood up against her family—they were very rich indeed and didn't believe in educating girls—and showed her passion by acting on what she believed, not preaching. I love the way she never outgrew some of her adolescent traits, remaining true to her politics— she was a self-taught socialist—throughout her life. I think I've read everything she wrote. I even called my daughter after her.

What kinds of music do you like?

I like all sorts of music, and I still listen to music I liked when I was seventeen. Neither of my parents was interested in classical music—they loved the Beatles and other sixties stuff, and I like those too. I played the acoustic guitar and would fantasize about playing an electric guitar solo. I still like the Beatles. My favorite group in all the world is the Smiths. And when I was going through a punky phase, it was the Clash.

Do you enjoy art?

I loved art at school and I still draw for pleasure. For some reason—maybe it was because I knew I would never make a living out of it—I never minded showing people my drawings and paintings. I never show my writing to anybody. My editor will tell you! I find it so hard to let go. It's too important. I hate it when people ask to see my rough drafts—they're too personal, somehow.

I love art galleries. I've now been to New York on book tours several times—it's one of my favorite places—and I've yet to visit any of the fabulous galleries there. I'm always desperate to go but there's never an afternoon free.

In my early twenties, I had a passion for Gainsborough, especially a painting called The Morning Walk. It is of the most extraordinary couple—the man is very striking while the woman is quite wishy-washy—and the explanation was that this painting was done for their marriage. I wondered how that marriage worked out and something told me it hadn't.

Perhaps my favorite painting is Caravaggio's Supper at Emmaus when Jesus reveals himself to the disciples having risen from the dead. I love it. Jesus looks very likeable—soft and rounded—and the painting captures the exact moment when the disciples realize who this man is, blessing their bread.

Did you go to the theatre or the cinema?

We went to pantomimes in London. I remember in one production of *Peter Pan* we were asked to hiss at Captain Hook, and Dad booed. Captain Hook came off the stage and all the way up to our seats—I was terrified.

I love going to the theatre now. The first play I saw was at Stratford upon Avon. It was a Sixth Form [corresponds to eleventh grade in the American system] outing and we saw Shakespeare's *King Lear*. I was absolutely electrified by it. We also saw *The Winter's Tale* and that was where I found the name Hermione—although of course it didn't come in handy until years later.

I like the cinema. There was no cinema in Chepstow so we didn't go much when I was a child. My favorite film then was *The Jungle Book*. I also liked the film of Richard Adams' *Watership Down*—of course, it's a wonderful book.

I think my favorite film star would probably be Michael Caine, although I had a massive crush on Dustin Hoffman after I saw him in *Little Big Man*. I've still got a bit of a thing about him. . . .

Did you watch much television as a child?

Not really. My parents wouldn't have the TV on much. I loved cartoons—I still do—especially *Wacky Races*. And I loved the Monkees—in fact I was in love with Davy Jones. When my daughter was very small I would ask her to call me when *Animaniacs* started on a Saturday morning, and she would come and bounce up and down on my bed to wake me up.

Recently, because I've been writing so much and away a lot, I've hardly watched television. Sometimes I've even missed important things on the news. I try never to miss *The Royle Family* though—that is a brilliant series.

MY CAREER

What did you do when you left school?

I went to Exeter University for four years, including a year teaching English in Paris which I loved. At first Exeter was a bit of a shock. I was expecting to be amongst lots of similar people—thinking radical thoughts. But it wasn't like that. However, once I'd made friends with some like-minded people I began to enjoy myself. Although I don't think I worked as hard as I could have.

Why did you choose to study languages when you loved English literature so much?

That was a bit of a mistake. I certainly didn't do everything my parents told me, but I think I was influenced by their belief that languages would be better for finding a job. I don't regret it hugely, but it was a strange decision for someone who only really wanted to be a writer, not that I'd had the courage to tell anyone that, of course.

Where did you go once you had graduated?

That was an even bigger mistake. I went to London to do a bilingual secretarial course (a course for secretaries who can speak more than one language). I was—am—totally unsuited to that kind of work. Me as a secretary? I'd be your worst nightmare.

But the one thing I did learn to do was to type. Now I type all my own books, so that's been incredibly useful. I'm pretty fast.

When I finished the course I just wanted to find a job—any job—that would earn a living to give me time to write. In fact, I landed a job with

Amnesty International as a research assistant into human rights abuses in Francophone, Africa (the part of Africa where people mainly speak French). It meant that I was working with representatives of over one hundred nationalities—all under the one roof. That made it a very, very interesting place to work, and worthwhile. If I wasn't writing full-time it was important that my time was being spent on something worthwhile.

I'm not sure that many of the people working there at the time would remember me, because at lunchtimes, when they were all off to the pub, I would make some kind of excuse and rush off to a café or another pub to write. I was working on an adult novel. I was sharing a flat at the time, and again, to get away, I would head for the local cafés. They were the ideal place to go and write—especially for someone who wasn't being honest about what she was up to. So that's how my passion for writing in cafés started.

MY CAREER

AS A WRITER

When did the idea for Harry Potter first enter your head?

My boyfriend was moving to Manchester and wanted me to move too. It was during the train journey back from Manchester to London, after a weekend looking for a flat, that Harry Potter made his appearance. I have never felt such a huge rush of excitement. I knew immediately that this was going to be such fun to write. I didn't know then that it was going to be a book for children—I just knew that I had this boy, Harry. During that journey I also discovered Ron, Nearly Headless Nick, Hagrid and Peeves. But with the idea of my life careering round my head, I didn't have a pen that worked! And I never went anywhere without my pen and notebook. So rather than trying to write it, I had to think it. And I think that was a very good thing. I was besieged by a mass of detail, and if it didn't survive that journey, it probably wasn't worth remembering.

Hogwarts School of Witchcraft and Wizardry was the first thing I concentrated on. I was thinking of a place of great order, but immense danger, with children who had skills with which they could overwhelm their teachers. Logically it had to be set in a secluded place, and pretty soon I settled on Scotland in my mind. I think it was in subconscious tribute to where my parents had married. People keep saying they know what I based Hogwarts on—but they're all wrong. I have never seen a castle anywhere that looks the way I imagine Hogwarts.

So I got back to the flat that night and began

to write it all down in a tiny cheap notebook. I wrote lists of all the subjects to be studied—I knew there had to be seven. The characters came first, and then I had to find names to fit them. Gilderoy Lockhart is a good example. I knew his name had to have an impressive ring to it. I was looking through the *Dictionary of Phrase and Fable*—a great source for names—and came across Gilderoy, a handsome Scottish highwayman. Exactly what I wanted. And then I found Lockhart on a war memorial to the First World War. The two together said everything I wanted about the character.

Can you describe the process of creating the stories?

It was a question of discovering why Harry was where he was, why his parents were dead. I was inventing it, but it felt like research. By the end of that train journey I knew it was going to be a seven-book series. I know that's extraordinarily arrogant for somebody who had never been published, but that's how it came to me. It took me five years to plan the series out, to plot through each of the seven novels. I know what and who's coming when, and it can feel like greeting old friends. Professor Lupin, who appears in the third book, is one of my favorite characters. He's a damaged person, literally and metaphorically. I think it's important for children to know that adults, too, have their problems, that they struggle. His being a werewolf is really a metaphor for people's reactions to illness and disability.

I almost always have complete histories for my characters. If I put all that detail in, each book would be the size of the *Encyclopaedia Britannica*, but I do have to be careful that I don't just assume that the reader knows as much as I do. Sirius Black is a good example. I have a whole childhood worked out for him. The readers don't need to know that but I do. I need to know much more than them because I'm the one moving the characters across the page.

I invented the game of Quidditch after a huge row with the boyfriend I lived with in Manchester. I stormed out of the house, went to the pub—and invented Quidditch.

Did you give up work to write the books?

Oh no! I moved to Manchester and worked for the Manchester Chamber of Commerce—rather briefly, because almost immediately I was made redundant. I then went to work at the university but I was really very unhappy. My mother had died about a month after I moved there. And then we were burgled, and everything my mother had left me was stolen. People were incredibly kind and friendly, but I decided that I wanted to get away.

I knew that I'd enjoyed teaching English as a foreign language in Paris and I thought to myself, how would it be if I went abroad, did some teaching, took my manuscript, had some sun . . . ? That's how I came to live in Oporto in Portugal, teaching students aged eight to sixty-two. They were mostly teenagers preparing for exams, but there were also business people and housewives. The teenagers aged between fourteen and seventeen years were easily my favorite. They were so full of ideas and possibilities, forming opinions. I became head of that department.

After six months, I met my husband-to-be, a journalist. We married, and the next year had Jessica—just before my twenty-eighth birthday. That was, without doubt, the best moment of my life. At that point, I had completed the first three chapters of *Harry Potter and the Philosopher's Stone*, almost exactly as they appear in the published book. The rest of the book was in rough draft.

Why did you move to Edinburgh?

It became clear that my marriage wasn't working, and I decided that it would be easier if I came back to Britain. My job wasn't tremendously secure, and of course it stopped completely over the summer holidays. I was worried about finding work during that period, especially with a small baby. I came to Edinburgh to stay with my sister for Christmas, and I thought, I can be happy here. And I have been.

The only people I knew in Edinburgh were my sister and her best friend. I'd only met my sister's husband once before. Most of my friends were in London, but I felt that Edinburgh was the kind of city in which I wanted to bring up my child. Pretty soon I made some good friends. Maybe it was my Scottish blood calling me home.

How did you continue to write?

I decided to return to teaching to earn a living,

but first I had to get the qualification—a Post-Graduate Certificate in Education. That would take a year, so I knew that unless I made a push to finish the first book now, I might never finish it. I made a huge, superhuman effort. I would put Jessica in her pushchair, take her to the park and try to tire her out. When she fell asleep I'd rush to a café and write. Not all the cafés I went to approved of me sitting there for a couple of hours having bought only one cup of coffee. . . . But my brother-in-law had just opened his own café—Nicolson's—and I thought they might be welcoming. I was careful to go when they weren't busy, and the staff were very nice. I used to joke about what I'd do for them if I ever got published and the book sold well. . . . I still wasn't sure that I'd ever be published. So my first book was finished in Nicolson's.

I typed the manuscript out on a manual typewriter. I'd read in the *Writers' and Artists' Year*

Book that the optimum length for a children's novel was 40,000 words—mine was 90,000! To try to disguise this, I typed it in single-line spacing (with the lines close together), but I didn't fool anybody. I had to type it all out again, double-line spaced (with the lines further apart). I'd sneak into the Open Access computers in college at weekends, or type with Jessica at my feet working her way through piles of jigsaws. I was terrified that people would discover that I wasn't doing my course work.

The first agent I sent the manuscript to returned it. The first publisher I sent the manuscript to returned it. So I sent it off again. The second agent, Christopher Little, took it on— his letter is one of the best I've ever received. It took a year to find a publisher but when Bloomsbury accepted it, it was definitely the second-best moment in my life—after Jessica.

A year later, July 1997, the book was

published—I walked around all day with a finished copy tucked under my arm. The first time I saw it in a bookshop I had this mad desire to sign it. It was an extraordinary moment. The first two words Jessica could read were "Harry" and "Potter," and she'd yell them out in bookshops. I was sure people would think I was making her do it. . . .

What happened after *Harry Potter and the Philosopher's Stone* was published?

My publisher was very encouraging and told me it was selling surprisingly well. There was no great fanfare—a good review in *The Scotsman*, followed by some others—but mostly it seems to have been word of mouth. Then my American publisher, Scholastic, bought the rights to the first book [where it was published as *Harry Potter and the Sorcerer's Stone*] for more money than anyone had expected. The burst of publicity terrified me. I was teaching part-time by then, and trying to write *Harry Potter and the Chamber of Secrets*. I felt frozen by all the attention.

What made you decide to become a full-time writer?

It wasn't an easy decision. I didn't know whether this was all just a flash in the pan. And I had my daughter to think of. But I thought that I could probably afford to write full-time for two years, although I was risking my teaching career because I wouldn't gain the experience necessary to go back to it as a career. When I won the Smarties Book Prize, sales started to climb. I got my first royalty check. I didn't expect to earn any royalties—not for a first novel—so that was a very proud moment.

It wasn't a great start, though, because I found *Harry Potter and the Chamber of Secrets* incredibly hard to finish. I was worried that it wouldn't live up to readers' expectations—I'd heard that your second novel is the hardest to write. In the end I delivered the manuscript on time but took it back for six weeks until I was satisfied with it.

Did you receive many letters from your readers?

I remember my first ever fan letter, from Francesca Gray. It began, "Dear Sir . . ." I've since met her. There was a growing trickle of mail, but when the book began to sell well in America the letters poured in. I realized that I was fast becoming my own inefficient secretary. It was a really nice problem to have, but it was time to hire someone to do things properly.

What happened when *Harry Potter and the Chamber of Secrets* was published?

It went almost straight to number one in the best-seller lists, which I thought was incredible. You have to remember that these things were taking me hugely by surprise. The fact is that it all happened very quickly but what mattered was that I had written a book I was proud of.

And *Harry Potter and the Prisoner of Azkaban*?

The idea that children would queue up in bookshops to buy copies of my books delighted me. But there are other more disconcerting sides to that level of publicity—having your photograph appear regularly in the papers is not something I ever anticipated.

But all the time, children are reading the books. And we know now that adults are reading the books, too. And they like them. That's what I remember when I'm feeling besieged.

Did the publicity quiet down?

No! I thought it must have reached saturation point—surely—but the announcement that the film rights for the first book had been bought by Warner Bros. increased press interest.

Are you happy about Harry Potter being made into a film?

I am now. We were inundated with offers from film companies, and I said no to all of them—even Warner. But they kept coming back. I'm not against the idea of a film—I love films. The vital thing for me was that it would be true to the book, and I have great faith in Warner's commitment to that. Obviously there are some things that won't "work" on screen, but I didn't want the plot to change very much at all. The decision to go with Warner wasn't about money or power, it was because I believed in them. I'd also seen their screen adaptations of *The Secret Garden* and *The Little Princess*, and I thought they were very good.

They've given me a lot of input, sent me maps and drawings of Hogwarts to make sure that when it appears on film it will be close to my vision of the place. The crucial thing is that the characters won't be led off in any inappropriate directions.

The thing I'm most looking forward to is seeing Quidditch. I've been watching it in my head for nine years now—and finally I'll get to see it along with everybody else.

Did your editor at Scholastic make many changes for the American edition?

Not very many at all. I read somewhere that the books had been "translated into American" and that's just nonsense. Changes were only made when words meant something completely different in America. A good example is "jumper." If I'd left that as it is in the British edition, Harry, Ron, and Fred would all have been wearing pinafore dresses as far as the American readers are concerned, and I was more than happy to substitute "sweater" to avoid that confusion! All Hagrid's dialect was left intact. The changes really were minimal.

The only thing I was uncomfortable about was that an American copy editor changed all the "mums" to "moms," and I just wasn't happy with that. Mrs. Weasley is not a "mom." So that's been reversed and they've been kept as "mums" for the other books.

What happened when you went to promote *Harry Potter and the Prisoner of Azkaban* in America?

On my previous tour, the greatest number of people at an event was probably about one hundred. My second tour began in Boston. As we were driving up to the bookshop I saw a massive queue snaking along two blocks. I asked Kris, from the publisher, Scholastic, if there was a sale on and she told me the queue was for me. It was the most extraordinary experience. They whisked me in the back entrance and took me upstairs, and when I walked through the door there was all this screaming and lots of flashbulbs going off. It was the nearest I'll ever come to being a pop star. I was totally speechless; I didn't know what to do with my face. I wanted to look friendly but I have a feeling I looked guilty and shifty. I signed one thousand four hundred books that day.

Do you enjoy the book tours?

The thing I enjoy best—apart from writing the books—is meeting the readers. Answering their questions is pure pleasure. This world that I've had in my head for years is now out there and in other peoples' heads! I love it. There are readers all over the world who are now intimate with characters that only I knew about until three years ago.

Your books have now been translated into at least 28 languages. What do you think of the different versions?

I've recently received copies of the first Harry translated into Japanese—it's beautiful. But I think the one I'm most impressed with is the Greek translation.

Sometimes I find strange little aberrations. In the Spanish translation Neville Longbottom's toad—which he's always losing—has been translated as a turtle. Which surely makes losing it rather more difficult. And there's no mention of water for it to live in. I don't want to think too much about that. . . . In the Italian translation, Professor Dumbledore has been translated into Professore Silencio. The translator has taken the "dumb" from the name and based the translation on that. In fact "dumbledore" is the Old English word for bumblebee. I chose it because my image is of this benign wizard, always on the move, humming to himself, and I loved the sound of the word too. For me "Silencio" is a complete contradiction. But the book is very popular in Italy—so it obviously doesn't bother the Italians!

Do you think you'll finish all seven Harry Potter novels?

Absolutely—if only for myself.

What will you do once you've finished the seventh?

It will be the most incredible thing to finish the books. It will have been a very long time to spend with those characters in my head and I know I'll be sad to leave them. But I know I will leave them alone.

I'm sure I'll always write, at least until I lose my marbles. I'm very, very lucky. Because of Harry's success, I don't need to do it financially, nobody's making me. I just need to do it for myself. Sometimes I think I'm temperamentally suited to being a moderately successful writer, with the focus of attention on the books rather than on me. It was wonderful enough just to be published. The greatest reward is the enthusiasm of the readers.

There are times—and I don't want to sound ungrateful—when I would gladly give back some of the money in exchange for time and peace to write. That's been the greatest strain, especially during the writing of the fourth book. I've become famous, and I'm not very comfortable with that. Because of the fame some really difficult things have happened, and it's required a great effort of will to shut them out. And I've also had to juggle the pressure to promote each book with the pressure from readers—and myself—to finish the next one. There have been some black weeks when I've wondered whether it's worth it. But I've ploughed on, and book four is exactly what I want it to be.

If you look at any famous person, there are always problems attached and they're not pleasant. But I still know that I'm an extraordinarily lucky person, doing what I love best in all the world.

J. K. ROWLING'S
BOOKS

An overview

Muggles, dementors, Quidditch, Knuts, the Whomping Willow—if these words sound alien to you, then you have yet to be introduced to the world of Harry Potter and his friends. And his enemies.

Since *Harry Potter and the Philosopher's Stone* was published in 1997 [and in the U.S.A. as *Harry Potter and the Sorcerer's Stone* in 1998], the world that J. K. Rowling first imagined during a train journey from Manchester to London one Sunday evening has become familiar to millions of people throughout the world. The stunning and rapid success of her books is unprecedented, drawing readers into two co-existing worlds—the ordinary Muggle world of humans and the extraordinary world of magic.

But just who is Harry Potter?

Because this book is being published with only four of J. K. Rowling's planned seven books in print, it is true to say that nobody, with the exception of the author, knows exactly who Harry Potter is.

We do know various things about him. We know that he is an orphan, that he survived the murderous intentions of the evil wizard Voldemort, and that he did not know, until he was eleven years old, that he was a wizard. There were a few indications that Harry was no ordinary boy. For example, his hair grew long overnight, not quite covering the mysterious lightning-shaped scar on his forehead, defying even the most brutal of haircuts. And there was the time, during a visit to the zoo, that a conversation with a Brazilian boa constrictor resulted in the snake gliding to freedom hissing, "Brazil, here I come. . . . Thanksss, amigo." Nobody was more surprised by this than Harry, and he was instantly blamed for it. As far as his uncle Vernon is concerned, everything that isn't normal is Harry's fault, and Uncle Vernon hates anything that isn't completely normal.

The opening of the first novel about Harry, *Harry Potter and the Sorcerer's Stone,* makes that aversion to anything out of the ordinary absolutely clear.

> *Mr. and Mrs. Dursley, of number four, Privet Drive, were proud to say that they were perfectly normal, thank you very much. They were the last people you'd expect to be involved in anything strange or mysterious, because they just didn't hold with such nonsense.*

Vernon and Petunia Dursley were forced to look after their nephew when he was abandoned on their doorstep as a baby, accompanied by a letter which presumably explained his tragic circumstances. They were horrified by the discovery and made Harry live in the cupboard under the stairs, treating him appallingly, in contrast to the overwhelming, blind devotion they showed to their odious son, Dudley.

For his first eleven years, Harry had no idea whatsoever that he was special. His aunt and uncle told him that his parents had died in a car crash. They were unfailingly unpleasant to him, and went out of their way to exclude him from treats or family events.

The truth is that Vernon and Petunia Dursley were terrified of Harry. They knew in their heart of hearts that he must be powerful, and that scared them. Even before he came to live with them they tried desperately to avoid facing the truth about

Mrs. Dursley's family. Mr. Dursley's reaction to a conversation he overhears about the Potters and their son, Harry, shows that the problem is rarely far from his mind.

> Mr. Dursley stopped dead. Fear flooded him. He looked back at the whisperers as if he wanted to say something to them, but thought better of it.
>
> He dashed back across the road, hurried up to his office, snapped at his secretary not to disturb him, seized his telephone, and had almost finished dialing his home number when he changed his mind. He put the receiver back down and stroked his mustache, thinking. . . no, he was being stupid. Potter wasn't such an unusual name. He was sure there were lots of people called Potter who had a son called Harry.

Once Harry has come to live with them, the need to disguise the truth increases. But with every day that passes they know that the time will come when he must discover his true identity—or at least some clues toward it. Although it is impossible not to despise the Dursleys, it's important to remember how frightened they must have been. So frightened that they could never discuss the situation sensibly with each other. It is as if by mentioning Harry's parents or his past, or what and who he is, they would be allowing themselves to think the unthinkable. Harry is their worst nightmare—the living evidence of a terrible family secret. And he's living right there in their home.

When you compare that picture with the reality of the kind of boy Harry is, the Dursleys seem terribly sad people. Ironically, their stupidity and cruelty have prevented them from having a normal home life. True, they dote on Dudley. But only to keep him quiet and content—and that never lasts for long. Harry, as we discover, isn't an angel. Like any boy, he can misbehave and disobey, but he is great fun, and the Dursleys miss out completely on that side of his character. Harry, for his part, comes to expect their mistreatment. It is only after his first year at Hogwarts School of Witchcraft and Wizardry, when he has made good friends and enjoyed being one of the crowd, that he realizes how miserable he has been with the Dursleys. That first summer holiday back at Privet Drive must have been dreadful, now that he knew how enjoyable and exciting life could be. Because he didn't realize that his mail was being intercepted by his uncle and aunt, he also thought his new friends had forgotten all about him. Knowing what he was missing must have made life even worse.

He missed Hogwarts so much it was like having a constant stomachache.

Of course, the Dursleys aren't the only people who are scared of Harry and his powers. We don't yet know exactly how Harry survived the attack which killed his parents, but survive it he did, marked with the distinctive lightning-shaped scar on his forehead. His would-be murderer is left weakened and angry—the worst kind of enemy to have. Even Albus Dumbledore, the wisest wizard of them all, doesn't fully understand. When Professor McGonagall asks him about the shocking death of Harry's parents, Lily and James, he can find no explanation.

"They're saying he [Voldemort] tried to kill the Potters' son, Harry. But—he couldn't. He couldn't kill that little boy. No one knows why, or how, but they're saying that when he couldn't kill Harry Potter, Voldemort's power somehow broke—and that's why he's gone."

Dumbledore nodded glumly.

"It's—it's true!" faltered Professor McGonagall. "After all he's done . . . all the people he's killed . . . he couldn't kill a little boy? It's just astounding . . . of all

the things to stop him . . . but how in the name of
heaven did Harry survive?"

"We can only guess," said Dumbledore, "we may
never know."

Harry's story is a very sad one. He has lost his parents and is utterly unloved by his relatives. He hasn't experienced much kindness at all in his first eleven years. Yet he is already celebrated. Just another little boy in the Muggle world, he is renowned in the world to which he was born—the magical world which exists alongside the ordinary lives of the Muggles. In that world he is Harry Potter— "the boy who lived!"

Darker moments

When J. K. Rowling first thought of the Harry Potter stories, she didn't see them primarily as books for children. Perhaps that's why she made no effort to simplify them. Their complications, twists and turns, red herrings, comedy, danger, and extraordinary special effects only add to the excitement. The author knew from the beginning that they were going to be fun to write and that has made them fun to read too, even during the darkest, most frightening moments. Who will ever forget Harry's first encounter with a dementor in *Harry Potter and the Prisoner of Azkaban*?

> *Its face was completely hidden beneath its hood. Harry's eyes darted downward, and what he saw made his stomach contract. There was a hand protruding from the cloak and it was glistening, grayish, slimy-looking and scabbed, like something dead that had decayed in water. . . .*

Later in the book, he discovers why his reaction to that horrible sight is so much more extreme than anybody else's.

Or what about the tense moments while Harry sits awaiting the decision of the Sorting Hat, a "patched and frayed and extremely dirty" pointed wizard's hat? Like every other new pupil at Hogwarts, Harry has to put on the hat to discover which house he will be joining—Gryffindor, Hufflepuff, Ravenclaw, or the dreaded Slytherin.

"Hmm," said a small voice in his ear. "Difficult. Very difficult. Plenty of courage, I see. Not a bad mind either. There's talent, oh my goodness, yes—and a nice thirst to prove yourself, now that's interesting. . . . So where shall I put you?"

Fortunately for Harry, the Sorting Hat decides on Gryffindor, but for a moment it is touch and go, and Harry never forgets how close he came to joining Slytherin. There is definitely something that connects him to the darker side of magic. It is evident too when he finally succeeds in finding the perfect wand, an "unusual combination—holly and phoenix feather, eleven inches, nice and supple." The salesman, a rather creepy gentleman, draws Harry's attention to a chilling coincidence.

> *Mr. Ollivander fixed Harry with his pale stare.*
>
> *"I remember every wand I've ever sold, Mr. Potter. Every single wand. It so happens that the phoenix whose tail feather is in your wand, gave another feather—just one other. It is very curious indeed that you should be destined for this wand when its brother— why, its brother gave you that scar."*

Harry's friends and other characters

The friendship between Harry, Ron, and Hermione is very important in the Harry Potter books. The two boys are not especially charitable toward Hermione to begin with, thinking her pushy and overenthusiastic about the academic side of life at Hogwarts. But eventually they realize that she is well worth including in their adventures, not least because she is very brave, as well as brainy. The three of them may have magic powers, but their friendship is very much like any other friendship between young people. They bicker and tease, but ultimately they know they can count on one another. After a particularly riveting lesson in which some of the pupils learn to confront their worst fear by making a Boggart take its shape and then laughing at it, Hermione declares her approval for the teacher, and the subject.

> *"But I wish I could have had a turn with the Boggart—"*
>
> *"What would it have been for you?" said Ron, sniggering. "A piece of homework that only got nine out of ten?"*

The teachers at Hogwarts are all fascinating

individuals. They know that Harry Potter is special, but they react in very different ways. Albus Dumbledore and Professor McGonagall, the headmaster and deputy headmistress, do their best to treat him fairly, sometimes even sparing him punishments because they believe that he has acted with the best of intentions, if not always wisely. Snape, on the other hand, loathes Harry and does his best to cause him harm and undermine his popularity. Sometimes it is hard to know exactly where some of the teachers stand in relation to the extraordinary young wizard in their midst. Professor Lupin, a teacher of Defense Against the Dark Arts, begins as a mysterious character, sound asleep on the Hogwarts train. There are no clues as to whether he will be a good or bad influence on the lives of Harry and his friends. As the story unfolds and the author begins to shed light on his character, we learn that he is far from straightforward, and that he has his own battles to fight.

The vast, disheveled Hagrid, expelled from Hogwarts in his youth for misuse of his magic powers, is an important ally for Harry. He might not be the brightest of friends, but he is tremendously loyal in return for the loyalty that Harry, Ron, and Hermione show him, often in the face of compelling evidence of his guilt.

Hagrid is also a great source of comedy. Apart from his fondness for inappropriate pets and an occasional overindulgence in alcohol—heartily disapproved of by Hermione—he has his own dialect. It is never more distinctive than when he is excited, as he is when he discovers that the Dursleys have never told Harry about his parents, and about how they died. He realizes that he is going to have to break the terrible news to their son by himself.

"It begins, I suppose, with—with a person called— but it's incredible yeh don't know his name, everyone in our world knows—"

"Who?"

"Well—I don' like sayin' the name if I can help it. No one does."

"Why not?"

"Gulpin' gargoyles, Harry, people are still scared. Blimey, this is difficult. See, there was this wizard who went . . . bad. As bad as you could go. Worse. Worse than worse. His name was . . ."

Then there is Dobby, the endlessly self-reproaching house-elf who tries his best to dissuade Harry from returning to Hogwarts for the start of his second year, always speaking of himself in the third person, and of Harry—to Harry—by his full name.

"Ah, sir," he gasped, dabbing his face with a corner of the grubby pillowcase he was wearing. "Harry Potter is valiant and bold! He has braved so many dangers already! But Dobby has come to protect Harry Potter, to

warn him, even if he does have to shut his ears in the oven doors later. . . . Harry Potter must not go back to Hogwarts."

The scale of the cast of characters controlled by J. K. Rowling is most impressive, and the success of the books proves that children can and do revel in complex plots and settings as long as they are gripped by the story. They love a challenge. Bloomsbury, the publishers of the Harry Potter books in the UK, produced special editions of the books for adult readers because they recognized that they were being widely read by parents of young readers keen to find out what the fuss was about. Perhaps surprised to find a so-called "children's book" so absorbing, they then recommended them to their friends. There is no difference in the story, however, only in the look of the book—the image on the jacket and the blurbs on the back cover.

Magic games and magic books

Perhaps it is because J. K. Rowling disliked hockey so intensely at school that she invented the exhilarating game of Quidditch, which plays such a crucial part in every Harry Potter book so far. Harry is an unlikely sporting hero—he is quite small and wears glasses—but his quick thinking and nimbleness, combined with the magical powers of his Quidditch broom, make him Gryffindor's secret weapon in the endless quest to win House points. Every Quidditch match has an additional element—other scores to settle—so that there is always more at stake than the match score at the end.

J. K. Rowling's passion for books and reading is also evident in the range of fascinating titles which make their appearance in her books. Hagrid sends Harry a biting book which is only brought under control by closing it forcibly with a belt. Tom

Riddle's magic diary plays a crucial part in the mystery at the heart of *Harry Potter and the Chamber of Secrets.* The reading list for all new Hogwarts pupils includes such intriguing titles as *Magical Theory* by Adalbert Waffling and *Magical Drafts and Potions* by Arsenius Jigger. And then of course there is that shameless self-publicist and best-selling author Gilderoy Lockhart—responsible for such deathless prose as *Gadding with Ghouls* and *Travels with Trolls,* among others, not forgetting his autobiography, the unsurprisingly titled *Magical Me.* It is only when his incompetence is rumbled by Harry and Ron that the truth about his authorship is revealed.

"So you've just been taking credit for what a load of other people have done?" said Harry incredulously.

"Harry, Harry," said Lockhart, shaking his head impatiently, "it's not nearly as simple as that. There was work involved. I had to track these people down. Ask them exactly how they managed to do what they did.

Then I had to put a Memory Charm on them so they wouldn't remember doing it. If there's one thing I pride myself on, it's my Memory Charms. . . ."

Moments later, Harry succeeds in repelling one of Lockhart's Memory Charms with the quick-thinking use of a spell taught to him by Snape. Lockhart lands in a crumpled heap on the floor, his reputation in ruins.

Eager readers

There rests with J. K. Rowling a heavy responsibility to keep her readers regularly supplied with up-to-date Harry Potter books. It is worth reminding ourselves of the literary feat she has achieved, and the challenge she has set herself for the future, all the more daunting because of the standards she has established in her first books. It is always hard, as a reader, to wait patiently for the next in a compelling series, but if we must wait, we can always re-read the previous books knowing that there is so much in them to enjoy. After J. K. Rowling's appearance at the Edinburgh International Book Festival in 1999, many of the Harry Potter books she was being asked to sign were almost worn out with re-reading and the questions asked by members of the audience showed an astonishing and impressive knowledge of the books. She was subjected to an in-depth interrogation by her readers—something she clearly loves.

But as the pompous Lockhart says, with rather less justification than his creator, "It's not all book signings and publicity photos, you know. You want fame, you have to be prepared for a long hard slog."

THE FOURTH BOOK

Harry Potter and the Goblet of Fire is the fourth book out of the seven-book series and therefore the one central in the story of Harry and his destiny. We find the darkest and scariest moment in the Harry Potter books so far in Voldemort's senseless and heartless killings.

A swishing noise and a second voice, which screeched the words to the night: "Avada Kedavra!"

A blast of green light blazed through Harry's eyelids, and he heard something heavy fall to the ground beside him; the pain in his scar reached such a pitch that he retched, and then it diminished; terrified of what

he was about to see, he opened his stinging eyes. . . ."

Voldemort is Harry's truest enemy: He killed Harry's parents, and he gave Harry the scar on his forehead, which blinds Harry with pain whenever Voldemort is near. He is the enemy who Harry's had to fight in all of the books of the series, but something about the words at the end of *Goblet of Fire:* "Lord Voldemort had risen again," tells us that Harry's battle is only going to get more intense.

Voldemort might dominate the action of *Harry Potter and the Goblet of Fire* if it weren't for the Quidditch World Cup and the Triwizard Tournament. The book opens with the World Cup final between Ireland and Bulgaria—an event filled with all the pure energy of a sports final like the Super Bowl, and all of the excitement and magic that you'd expect from the world of Harry Potter. And along with the Quidditch Cup, there is the

Triwizard Tournament. As Dumbledore explains:

> *"The Triwizard Tournament was first established some seven hundred years ago as a friendly competition between the three largest European schools of wizardry: Hogwarts, Beauxbatons, and Durmstrang. A champion was selected to represent each school, and the three champions competed in three magical tasks. . . . It was generally agreed to be a most excellent way of establishing ties between young witches and wizards of different nationalities—until, that is, the death toll mounted so high that the tournament was discontinued."*

In the Triwizard Tournament's first year back, Harry and Cedric Diggory are chosen to be champions from Hogwarts to compete in the three tasks that will challenge all of their wizarding skills.

In this fourth book, along with Cedric, two other characters who had their introduction in the first three books become much more important to

Harry: Cho Chang and Sirius Black. Cho is not one of the Harry, Ron, and Hermione trio, but she has an important role in the Harry Potter books because she is Harry's first crush. Harry asks her to the Yule Ball with him and is disappointed when he finds out she's already been asked by someone else.

Sirius Black, Harry found out in *Prizoner of Azkaban,* is his godfather, and only recently a criminal in the dreaded dementor jail, Azkaban. But Harry discovers that Sirius was wrongly sent away, and their relationship in *Goblet of Fire* quickly becomes one of trust and even love. Molly Weasley, Ron's mother, does everything to treat Harry like one of her own sons, knitting one of her famous Christmas sweaters and worrying about him constantly, but it's Sirius who feels to Harry like the parent he never had. Like Sirius, the people most important to Harry gather all that more closely to his side by the end of *Goblet of Fire,* as the story hints at the important events to come that will test

Harry, and to see how brave the "boy who lived" really is.

Harry Potter and the Goblet of Fire, the fourth and central book to the Harry Potter series, was so important to J. K. Rowling that she asked that it be released simultaneously in the English-speaking countries around the world, including the U.S.A., England, and Canada, on July 8, 2000. Children and adults lined up at bookstores to buy their first copies of the book, and J. K. Rowling sat down with *Entertainment Weekly, Newsweek, O, The Oprah Magazine,* and *Larry King Live,* and had a telephone conference with *The Plain Dealer,* to share some of her thoughts on the phenomenon of the fourth and pivotal book in the Harry Potter series.

NEWSWEEK: Has the mania reached a peak?
ROWLING: I don't know. I thought it had

reached a peak with *Prisoner of Azkaban,* and it hadn't. We can't carry on like this forever. At some point things have got to calm down. The film isn't going to help in terms of diminishing it.

NEWSWEEK: Has your success placed restrictions on your life? Can you walk down the street, go shopping?

ROWLING: Oh, yeah, absolutely. It's really the exception rather than the norm that anyone would approach me. I don't think I'm very recognizable, which I am completely happy to say. Further, no one has ever been less than completely charming when they've come up to me. And they tend to come up, obviously, if they've read the book, or their child has read the book, to tell me something very nice. There was a phase when I had journalists at my front door quite a lot, and that was quite horrible. That was not something I had ever anticipated happening to me, and it's not pleasant, whoever you are. But I don't want to whine, because this was my life's ambition, and I've over-shot the mark so hugely.

NEWSWEEK: Will [*Harry Potter and the Goblet of Fire*] be the biggest?

ROWLING: No, I think book seven will be. Seven's going to be like the *Encyclopaedia Britannica,* because I'm going to want to say good-bye. I always knew four would be a long one, but I didn't know it would be this long. But it had to be. I've got no regrets. That's how many words it took to tell the story I needed to tell. I like it. I'm very pleased with it. It's definitely the book that gave me the most trouble. But then *Chamber of Secrets* gave me a fair amount of trouble. Bizarrely, it seems that the two that were the most hell to write were the two I like the best.

NEWSWEEK: Have you thought about life after Harry Potter?

ROWLING: I definitely have thought about it, but I've made no decisions at all. I will definitely be writing. I literally don't quite feel right if I haven't written for a while. A week is about as long as I can go without getting extremely edgy. It's like a fix. It really is a compulsion. Yeah, so I have ideas, but they could be all rubbish.

O, THE OPRAH MAGAZINE: You admire Roddy Doyle and Jane Austen—both of whom write about class distinctions. You do in Harry Potter, too. Was that a conscious decision?

ROWLING: Well, a German journalist said to me, "There's a lot about money in the Harry Potter books." And I had never really thought about that before. But kids are acutely aware of money—before they're even aware of class. A kid isn't really going to notice how another kid holds his knife and fork. But a kid will be acutely aware that he doesn't have pocket money. Or that he doesn't have as much pocket money. I think back to myself at eleven. Kids can be mean, very mean. So it was there in Ron not having the proper length robes, you know? And not being able to buy stuff on the trolley. He's got to have sandwiches his mum made for him, even though he doesn't like the sandwiches. Having enough money to fit in is an important facet of life—and what is more conformist than a school?

O: With so much on your plate, when do you find time to read?

ROWLING: I never need to find time to read. When people say to me, "Oh, yeah, I love reading. I would love to read, but I just don't have time," I'm thinking, How can you not have time? I read when I'm drying my hair. I read in the bath. I read when I'm sitting in the bathroom. Pretty much anywhere I can do the job one-handed, I read.

LARRY KING: But how has all the success affected you? It has to affect you.

ROWLING: It has. Obviously, it's had a massive impact. Day to day not much. People might be surprised to hear that, but my day is really very—what it always was, which is trying to get time to write, which used to be difficult because I'm a single parent and I was doing a day job. And now it's difficult because the phone never stops ringing so I still walk out of the house to write. Occasionally, obviously, you know, I'm on the *Larry King* show. This was not a feature of my life.

LARRY KING: You also don't have economic pressure anymore.

ROWLING: I don't have economic pressure anymore. And every day people constantly say to me what's the best thing about that, and without a doubt the best thing is I don't have to worry. I mean, every day—you know, there will be single mothers out there who, I think, will really understand this: Nothing means more to me than the fact I don't have to worry about that anymore because it's a difficult way to live.

ROWLING: I never really have to psych myself up for writing. Normally, [the story] is pretty much there, although on Book Four, Chapter Nine . . . I rewrote that thirteen times. It half killed me.

ROWLING: . . .What's very important for me is when Dumbledore says that you have to choose between what is right and what is easy. This is the setup for the next three books. All of them are going to have to choose, because what is easy is often not right.

ENTERTAINMENT WEEKLY: What do you like about the States?

ROWLING: Well, what don't I like about it? I really, really, *really* fell in love with New York. The first signing I did over there, the first boy to reach me in the queue put out his hand and went "YOU ROCK!" I thought that was great, but I heard myself respond and I sounded so intensely British, something like "That's *very* nice of you to say so, thank you so much." Then there was this woman in L.A., a middle-aged sort of Palm Beach-type woman. She said, "I AM SO GLAD YOU'RE RICH!" I'm telling you, you'd *never* hear that in Britain. Here, it's "*Well done.*"

BIBLIOGRAPHY
In date order

HARRY POTTER AND THE SORCERER'S STONE · SCHOLASTIC 1998

Harry Potter thinks he is an ordinary boy—until he is rescued by a beetle-eyed giant of a man, enrolls at Hogwarts School of Witchcraft and Wizardry, learns to play Quidditch, and does battle in a deadly duel. The reason: HARRY POTTER IS A WIZARD!

Winner of the Smarties Book Prize Gold Award 1997; the British Book Awards Children's Book of the Year 1998; FCBG Children's Book Awards overall winner 1998; Young Telegraph Paperback of the Year Award 1998; Birmingham Cable Children's Book Award; Sheffield Children's Book Award; The Booksellers Association/The Bookseller Author of the Year 1998; American Booksellers Book Award 1999;

the Children's Book Prize 1999 of the "Jury of Young Readers" Vienna; Kinderboekwinkelprijs 1999; Permio Cento per la Letteratura Infantile 1998; Anne Spencer Libergh Prize in Children's Literature 1997–1998; Prix Sorcière 1999; Prix Tam-Tam "Je bouquine" 1999; *School Library Journal* Best Book of the Year; American Library Association Notable Book and Best Book for Young Adults 1998; *Publishers Weekly* Best Book of the Year; New York Public Library Best Book of the Year; *Parenting Magazine* Book of the Year Award 1998; Smithsonian Notable Books for Children; Borders Books Choice for 1999; *Booklist* Editors' Choice 1998; shortlisted for the Carnegie Medal (commended) 1998; the Guardian Fiction Prize 1998; Deutscher Jugendliteraturpreis 1999

HARRY POTTER AND THE CHAMBER OF SECRETS

• SCHOLASTIC 1999

Harry Potter, the wizard, is in his second year at Hogwarts School of Witchcraft and Wizardry. Little does he know that this year will be just as eventful as the last. . . .

Winner of the Smarties Book Prize Gold Award 1998; the British Book Awards Children's Book of the Year 1999; FCBG Children's Book Awards 1999; Scottish Arts Council Children's Book Award 1999; North East Book Award; North East Scotland Book Award; American Library Association Notable Book and Best Book for Young Adults 1999; *Booklist* Editors' Choice 1999; *School Library Journal* Best Book of the Year 1999; shortlisted for the Whitbread Children's Book of the Year Award 1999; the Sheffield Children's Book Award; the Guardian Fiction Prize 1999

HARRY POTTER AND THE PRISONER OF AZKABAN

• SCHOLASTIC 1999

Harry Potter, along with his best friends, Ron and Hermione, is about to start his third year at Hogwarts School of Witchcraft and Wizardry. He can't wait to get back to school after the summer holidays. (Who wouldn't if they lived with the horrible Dursleys?) But when Harry gets to Hogwarts, the atmosphere is tense. There's an escaped mass murderer on the loose, and the sinister prison guards of Azkaban have been called in to guard the school. . . .

Winner of the Whitbread Children's Book of the Year Award 2000; the British Book Awards Children's Author of the Year 2000; the Smarties Book Prize Gold Award 1999; American Library Association Notable Book and Best Book for Young Adults 2000; *Los Angeles Times* Best Book 1999; *Booklist* Editors' Choice 2000; shortlisted for the Carnegie Medal

HARRY POTTER AND THE GOBLET OF FIRE · SCHOLASTIC 2000

Before Harry Potter goes back to the wizard school Hogwarts for his fourth year, he gets to go to the Quidditch World Cup. But there he sees the first indication that Voldemort is coming ever closer, and with the Triwizard Tournament taking place for the first time in years, everyone is on the lookout for trouble. . . .

Shortlisted for the British Book Awards Children's Book of the Year 2000; *Publishers Weekly* Best Children's Books of 2000; Smithsonian Notable Children's Books 2000; Amazon.com Editors' Choice selection, ages 9–12; *Booklist* Editors' Choice 2000; ALA Notable Children's Book 2000

About the interviewer

Lindsey Fraser is a leading children's book enthusiast. She started work in James Thin Booksellers in Edinburgh, Scotland, before managing Heffers Children's Bookshop in Cambridge, England. She is now Executive Director of Scottish Book Trust, an organization renowned for its work in promoting reading among children and in raising the profile of children's literature.